DIVORCE RECOVERY

PICKING UP THE PIECES

Serendipity House / P.O. Box 1012 / Littleton, CO 80160

TOLL FREE 1-800-525-9563 / www.serendipityhouse.com

99 00 01 02 / **101 video series • CHG** / 4 3 2 1

PROJECT ENGINEER
Lyman Coleman

WRITING TEAM
Richard Peace, William Cutler, Andrew Sloan, Cathy Tardif

VIDEO DIRECTOR
Barry Deardorff

VIDEO TECHNICAL SUPPORT
Doug Anderson and Colorful Concepts Studios

CARTOONS
Robert Schull

PRODUCTION TEAM
Christopher Werner, Sharon Penington, Erika Tiepel
The Serendipity Staff

ACKNOWLEDGMENTS

To Zondervan Bible Publishers
for permission to use
the NIV text, and Bible study notes
The Holy Bible, New International Bible Society.
© 1973, 1978, 1984 by International Bible Society.
Used by permission of Zondervan Bible Publishers.

Questions and Answers

1. **What is unique about this course?** The combination of three activities in one integrated program:
   - ❐ Video Presentation
   - ❐ Interaction in Small Groups
   - ❐ Bible Study

2. **Who is it for?**
   - ❐ Churches
   - ❐ Schools
   - ❐ Community organizations

3. **Where can I use this program?**
   - ❐ Classrooms with movable chairs / TV
   - ❐ One-day seminars
   - ❐ Weekend retreats
   - ❐ Courses from seven to thirteen weeks

4. **How long is each session?** 90 minutes.

5. **What if I do not have 90 minutes?** Divide the session into two sessions, making the course 13 weeks instead of seven.

6. **How much does the course leader have to know about the subject?** Very little. The video presents the material. The leader convenes the meeting and follows the agenda.

7. **What about the group interaction?** This is directed by a HANDOUT which each person is given at the beginning of the session for the three times the group shares. The HANDOUT needs to be photocopied for every member.
   - ❐ Ice-Breaker—to start the session and divide the class into groups of 4 to 6 for sharing (Side One of HANDOUT)
   - ❐ Respond to Video—in same groups (Side One of HANDOUT)
   - ❐ Respond to Bible Study—in same groups (Side Two of HANDOUT)

8. **Why do you divide into groups of 4 to 6?** To allow everyone to share.

9. **How would you go about dividing the class?** Divide the number of participants in the class by 4 to 6 to determine the number of groups needed. Then, ask the class to count off—1, 2, 3, etc.

10. **Would you have the same groups meet every session?** That is up to you. There are advantages both ways.

11. **How does this course fit into the larger educational structures of the church?** This is an entry level, short-term group for people with special needs or specific interest.

12. **Can this group continue as an ongoing small group after this course is over?** Yes. In the last session, the group is encouraged to make a contract or covenant for another 7 to 13 weeks, and move on to deeper Group Bible Study. A full description of the ongoing 201 Study courses are described inside the back cover.

13. **Are there other video courses available?** Yes. For a complete curriculum of courses for small groups in the church, call Serendipity at 1-800-525-9563.

CHECKLIST BEFORE THE SESSION

❑ EQUIPMENT: TV, VCR, sound system (if more than 10–12 people in the session).

❑ ROOM ARRANGEMENT: Movable chairs for subdividing into groups of 4 to 6.

❑ HANDOUTS: Every person needs a Handout for every session. Permission is given for you to photocopy the Handout as needed. Remember, there are two sides to each Handout.

❑ SPLIT SESSIONS: If you want to divide a session because you do not have 90 minutes, there is an ice-breaker to kick off the second part which you will need to photocopy from this book and give to the class.

❑ BIBLES: The Bible passage for discussion has been included in the Handout. However, if you want the class to read from their own Bibles, ask the people in the class to bring their Bibles.

❑ LEADER BOOK: Be sure to bring the book to the session and follow the agenda for each part of the session.

4

Agenda for Each Session

15 Minutes	**ICE-BREAKER / Groups of 4 to 6** Divide the class into subgroups of 4 to 6 for a few minutes to get acquainted and unpack before turning on the video. Give the HAND-OUT—Side One to everyone. You have permission to photocopy the HANDOUT (both sides) for the session as needed.
10 Minutes	**VIDEO / All Together** Bring the subgroups back together to watch the Video for the session.
30 Minutes	**RESPOND TO VIDEO / Groups of 4 to 6** Regather in groups of 4 to 6 (same groups) to answer the questions on the HANDOUT (Side One) about the Video.
30–45 Minutes	**BIBLE STUDY / Same Groups of 4 to 6** *Option 1:* If you have a full 90 minutes for a session, follow the three-part agenda. *Option 2:* If you only have 60 minutes for the session, do the Bible study at the next session. A separate Ice-Breaker is provided for this Bible study—which you will need to photocopy for class members.

"DIVORCE IS A LOSS OF MONUMENTAL PROPORTIONS...
UNFORTUNATELY... WE HAVE NO CLEAR PROCESS
FOR MOURNING A 'DEAD' MARRIAGE...."

Mourning the Former Life

OBJECTIVES

To begin to get to know each other, and to share who we are.

To relate our divorce experiences to what commonly occurs in a mourning / grieving process.

To look at a scriptural incident of personal loss and see what it says to us about the nature of mourning.

THREE-PART AGENDA

ICE-BREAKER
15 Minutes

VIDEO / RESPONSE
45 Minutes

BIBLE STUDY
30–45 Minutes

OPTION: If you only have 60 minutes, divide this session into two sessions, with the Bible Study section for your next time together.

ICE-BREAKER

Pass out the Handout for this session and divide the class into groups of 4 to 6 to get acquainted before showing the video. Photocopy pages 10 and 12 as needed so that each person has their own Handout.

1. Give your name and tell what you would probably be doing if you weren't here in this group at this time.

2. Choose one of the following couples you enjoyed watching on TV. What expectation did they give you of how marriage should be?
   ❏ Ward and June Cleaver (*Leave It to Beaver*)
   ❏ Steve and Alyse Keeton (*Family Ties*)
   ❏ Rob and Laura Petry (*Dick Van Dyke Show*)
   ❏ Cliff and Clair Huxtable (*Cosby Show*)
   ❏ Archie and Edith Bunker (*All in the Family*)
   ❏ Tim and Jill Taylor (*Home Improvement*)
   ❏ other:_____

3. How long were you married and how long have you been divorced?

Ward and June Cleaver raising Wally and the Beaver in a nice home in a nice neighborhood—that's how many of us see the dream of the American family. Ward and June never had fights (well, not any serious ones, anyway!), all the problems were solved in 30 minutes, and the kids with real problems all belonged to someone else. What a nice dream! But, it's far from most people's reality, and in the case of many of us, those who have gone through divorce, reality at times is more like a nightmare. Consider these two stories:

Marcia

Marcia thought she had a pretty good marriage. True, there were a few things that didn't seem quite right, and her husband John seemed to spend a lot of extra time at work. But she was happy and her husband said that he was too—that is, until the day he didn't come home. Marcia discovered in her husband a pattern of deception over several months, deception that included another woman at work. He had left to be with her and Marcia was left to explain to two young girls that their father was not just gone on a long trip—he was not coming back at all.

Ken

Ken filed for a divorce after 13 years of marriage and a year and a half of marital counseling. He tore himself away from two crying children and went to live in a three-room apartment furnished only with a used bedroom set from a Motel 6, and a rickety dinette with two chairs. His children did visit, but oftentimes his only company was a couple of parakeets and dozens of cockroaches.

For thousands of people like Marcia and Ken, divorce is an earthquake that shatters our world and leaves nothing in its familiar place. Both Marcia and Ken had to mourn losses. Ken lost not only his marriage, but his home, daily contact with his children, his relationship with his former in-laws, and many of his friends. Marcia lost not only her husband, but a live-in father for her children, much of her financial stability and—perhaps most significantly—her view of reality and her confidence in her own perception of that reality.

Divorce: A loss to be mourned

Divorce is a loss of monumental proportions. It is often compared to mourning a spouse who has died. Some say it's harder; some say it's easier. It probably depends on the circumstances. But generally, the degree of pain in the two experiences is in the same ballpark. Unfortunately, while we have a formalized ritual for mourning a death, we have no clear process for mourning a "dead" marriage. Most people don't know how to react. Should we celebrate and throw a party? Or is a kind of divorce-wake more appropriate? Or should we try to go about life as if we were simply changing residences?

Divorced persons often have to mourn the loss of their marriage as if it were a death. That doesn't mean divorce never brings changes that should be welcomed and celebrated. It just means that before you can go on to what is ahead of you, you must mourn what is being left behind. That is true regardless of whether you initiated or resisted the divorce, and whether you see the divorce as something positive or something negative.

What then is the process for mourning such a loss? Dr. Elisabeth Kübler-Ross is famous for her five stages of mourning:
- Denial—we have difficulty facing the reality of what is happening.
- Anger—our hurt over the loss is ventilated in anger toward ourselves and/or others.
- Bargaining—we imagine we can change the reality by bargaining with God, our ex-spouse or whoever else might have relevance.
- Depression—we feel powerless to face the overwhelming reality.
- Acceptance—we adapt to the new reality.[1]

Other writers enumerate more stages than Kübler-Ross, but a growing trend is to see mourning as a process that cannot be neatly divided into stages. It does, however, involve certain consistently present aspects. Some of them are most often dealt with early in the process, while others often occur late in the process.

Making the transition
These feelings will never really "go away" until we come to terms with what is ending and actively move into a time of transition. Whether we welcomed the divorce or were dragged into it kicking and screaming, we have lost something vitally important.

Mourning takes time. Many divorced people want to know something they can do to keep from prolonging their pain. It doesn't work that way. Often it takes three to five years to fully adjust to a divorce. The most painful part of the mourning will probably take upward to a year. It may be helpful to think of this pain as labor pain. A new you is coming. But birth means labor, and you are in the midst of the labor pains that will bring the new you to birth.

How we respond will be determined in large part by whether or not we initiated the divorce and how we felt about it. People who choose their transitions minimize the pain of endings; those whose transitions are chosen for them find it hard to believe good will come out of the change.

Still, people who have gone through the death of a marriage, even unwillingly, often find that new life emerges on the other side. That new life may not be what one sees on *Leave It to Beaver,* but it's good, it's full of God's grace, and it's real.

Mourning the Former Life

☕ ICE-BREAKER / Groups of 4 to 6 / 15 Minutes

1. Give your name and tell what you would probably be doing if you weren't here in this group at this time.

2. Choose one of the following couples you enjoyed watching on TV. What expectation did they give you of how marriage should be?
   ❑ Ward and June Cleaver (*Leave It to Beaver*)
   ❑ Steve and Alyse Keeton (*Family Ties*)
   ❑ Rob and Laura Petry (*Dick Van Dyke Show*)
   ❑ Cliff and Clair Huxtable (*Cosby Show*)
   ❑ Archie and Edith Bunker (*All in the Family*)
   ❑ Tim and Jill Taylor (*Home Improvement*)
   ❑ other:_____

3. How long were you married and how long have you been divorced?

📺 RESPOND TO THE VIDEO / Same Groups / 30 Minutes

1. Place your own divorce experience somewhere along the following continuum, according to how much warning you had that it was coming:
   _____
   a bolt out of the blue (like Marcia)   **a long time coming (like Ken)**

2. What aspects of married life do you (or will you) miss the most?
   ❑ someone to talk to   ❑ going out
   ❑ a parent for my child(ren)   ❑ sharing responsibilities
   ❑ physical intimacy   ❑ my "married" identity
   ❑ my good reputation   ❑ other:_____

3. As you look back over your life, what other major life transitions have you experienced in the past few years? Did you choose them, or were they forced upon you?

4. If divorce recovery is like being in childbirth labor, where are you in the process?
   ❑ tired, miserable and overdue
   ❑ just beginning to feel contractions and knowing the worst is yet to come
   ❑ heading to the hospital and wondering if it's too late to back out
   ❑ having false labor—and I think it's twins!
   ❑ just wanting a shot for the pain, so it will go away
   ❑ ecstatic, because the new me is already emerging

The Bible passage we will be studying is not about divorce; it's about death. We are looking at it for two reasons. First, as mentioned in the video, experiencing divorce and experiencing the death of a loved one have some similarities in the intensity of the pain we feel. Second, this passage illustrates some of the stages of mourning which a person experiences in divorce.

The passage follows the death of David's son, Absalom. David's relationship with Absalom was not the kind of father-son relationship one would normally see on TV, except perhaps on *The Simpsons*. Absalom, quite frankly, was a self-serving spoiled brat. He sought to turn people against his father David, and even led a revolt to overthrow him. For that reason, when Absalom was killed by David's forces, most of the people thought that David would welcome the news. Perhaps he might not be happy (Absalom was, after all, his son), but he would at least be relieved. They forgot, however, two things. First, mourning is not a rational process. You may have lost what your mind says is no good for you, but your heart is slow to follow such logic. Second, they forgot that once the bonds of family are created, they are not easily broken.

We pick up the story when David learns of the death of Absalom from a Cushite soldier in his army.

> **ICE-BREAKER FOR TWO-SESSION OPTION**
> *If you are doing the Bible Study as a separate session, start off this session by dividing the class into small groups of 4 to 6 and answering these questions. Photocopy and give this to the group.*

Driver Education. Living life is like driving a car. Sometimes the ride is exhilarating. Sometimes it's excruciatingly slow. We often have no control over what other drivers are doing around us (and that can be frustrating), but we do have something to say about what we do behind the wheel—as long as we obey the traffic laws of course!

1. How was your ride last week?
    ❏ frantic—like the final lap of the Indy 500
    ❏ disastrous—totalled the car; had to be towed
    ❏ confusing—tried to go somewhere new and got lost
    ❏ smooth—like a relaxed Sunday drive
    ❏ bumpy—riding over major ruts and bumps
    ❏ stalled—couldn't even get out of the garage
    ❏ frightening—almost went over the edge
    ❏ other:_____

2. What was the most pleasant part of your ride last week?

SESSION ONE BIBLE STUDY

³¹Then the Cushite arrived and said, "My lord the king, hear the good news! The LORD has delivered you today from all who rose up against you." ³²The king asked the Cushite, "Is the young man Absalom safe?" The Cushite replied, "May the enemies of my LORD the king and all who rise up to harm you be like the young man." ³³The king was shaken. He went up to the room over the gateway and wept. As he went, he said: "O my son Absalom! My son, my son Absalom! If only I had died instead of you—O Absalom, my son, my son!"

19 *Joab was told, "The king is weeping and mourning for Absalom." ²And for the whole army the victory that day was turned into mourning, because on that day the troops heard it said, "The king is grieving for his son." ³The men stole into the city that day as men who steal in who are ashamed when they flee from battle. ⁴The king covered his face and cried aloud, "O my son Absalom! O Absalom, my son, my son!"*

⁵Then Joab went into the house to the king and said, "Today you have humiliated all your men, who have just saved your life and the lives of your sons and daughters and the lives of your wives and concubines. ⁶You love those who hate you and hate those who love you. You have made it clear today that the commanders and their men mean nothing to you. I see that you would be pleased if Absalom were alive today and all of us were dead. ⁷Now go out and encourage your men. I swear by the LORD that if you don't go out, not a man will be left with you by nightfall. This will be worse for you than all the calamities that have come upon you from your youth till now."

⁸So the king got up and took his seat in the gateway. When the men were told, "The king is sitting in the gateway," they all came before him.

2 Samuel 18:31–19:8

1. Why do you think David's anguish over his son's death was so intense?

2. If you had just risked your life to protect David, how would you have felt when you saw him weeping over the death of his son Absalom?

3. When have your feelings and responses about your ex-spouse confused your friends or family? What did you do? How did they respond?

4. When you mourn the end of your marriage (or its prospective end), what is it you are mourning?

5. When you feel your behavior (in regard to your divorce) is irrational, how do you respond?

2 Samuel 18:31–19:8

18:31 The Cushite soldier (a native of Cush or Ethiopia) brings news of the defeat of King David's enemies, led by his son, Absalom. The messenger assumes the king will be happy about the news, since Absalom had tried to kill David. But the Cushite has underestimated David's love for Absalom. Before Absalom was David's enemy he was David's son.

18:32 The obvious question for the king to ask is, "What happened?" But David is more concerned about the welfare of his son than his own army.

18:33 David, overwhelmed with grief upon hearing of his son's death, withdraws from public view, but not before making his grief obvious to those around him. His sobbing begins even before he is out of hearing range of the people. The narrator records David's constant repetition of his son's name, and his wish that he could have died in Absalom's place.

19:1 Word of David's grief reaches Joab, commander of the king's army, who not only has led the victory battle, but also killed Absalom with his own hands (see 18:14–15).

19:5 *Today you have humiliated all your men.* Joab doesn't pull any punches. He has an important perspective that David is unable to see. Joab realizes the devastating effect the king's grief is having on the troops' morale—and the real possibility they might abandon David. If Joab seems insensitive to David's grief, it is because he understands the seriousness of the situation and the king needs to be shocked back to his senses.

19:6 *You love those who hate you and hate those who love you.* By only grieving over his son (and not rejoicing over his own troops' victory), David leaves himself open to the charge that he loves his enemies more than his family, friends and soldiers. Joab forces David to face the painful, logical conclusions about his response to Absalom's death. In Joab's thinking, the choice was clear from the beginning: kill Absalom or be killed.

19:7 *Now go out.* Joab and David change roles. Now the captain of the army is giving orders to the king of the nation. Joab tells David precisely what he must do: commend and encourage his troops. To fail to do so, Joab warns, will be to risk having his entire army abandon him, and that would result in the worst disaster David has ever faced.

19:8 David follows Joab's instructions. He resumes his public duties in a visible place at the gateway of the city and all the troops come before him to receive his thanks and praise. David's time of mourning is by no means over. He has simply pulled himself together long enough to perform the functions of his public office.

"ULTIMATELY, WE HAVE TO LEARN TO FORGIVE THE EX-SPOUSE... EVERY OLD, UNFORGIVEN HURT IS A WEED THAT CAN CHOKE OUT NEW LIFE.."

The Continuing Conflict

To help us see that conflict and anger in divorce are normal.

To help us determine the most helpful ways of coping with conflict.

To consider how Jesus' command to love your enemies applies to divorce

THREE-PART AGENDA

ICE-BREAKER
15 Minutes

VIDEO / RESPONSE
45 Minutes

BIBLE STUDY
30–45 Minutes

OPTION: If you only have 60 minutes, divide this session into two sessions, with the Bible Study section for your next time together.

ICE-BREAKER

Pass out the Handout for this session and divide the class into groups of 4 to 6 to get acquainted before showing the video. Photocopy pages 18 and 20 as needed so that each person has their own Handout.

Adolescence is a period of transition, a time when a child gradually becomes a man or woman. That requires two things: the child must take more and more control of their life and the parent must exercise less and less control over the child. Therein lies lots of opportunity for conflict!

1. When you were a teenager, what was the most memorable conflict you had with your parents? What did you do to resolve this conflict?

2. In your normal style of handling conflict, which are you more like?
    ❐ an ostrich—I hide my head in the sand.
    ❐ the neighborhood bulldog—I challenge anyone who comes near my territory.
    ❐ a house dog—I timidly slouch away, then chew up the couch when no one's looking.
    ❐ a hawk—I fly above it all and pick my targets.
    ❐ a fox—I use my brains to win.
    ❐ a wolf—I am ferocious when cornered.
    ❐ a dolphin—I can fight if necessary, but would rather swim away.
    ❐ other:_____

Comparing divorce to death only goes so far. After all, there are some very important differences. A dead person doesn't phone you from time to time, doesn't demand child visitation rights, and will never show up at an event with a new boyfriend or girlfriend.

Jim Smoke, an author and singles minister, writes, "Divorce, unlike death, does not fully remove the ex-spouse from daily existence. Ex-spouses hover about the edges of a marriage dissolution and frequently wreck havoc with the other mate's life."[2]

How can you begin to recover from divorce when the presence of your ex-spouse continues to rub against the emotional and spiritual sores you need to heal? This question raises several more:
- How do you act in the midst of intense conflict when you have been taught that you should always be caring and forgiving?
- How do you stand up for your rights without getting into a childish fight?
- How do you express your feelings without doing a destructive act you will later regret?

The raging post-divorce whirlpool seems to sweep us along in its violence, and there sometimes seems to be no way out.

Sue
Sue had a long history of getting involved with men she later described as "losers," and her latest husband was no exception. He couldn't keep a job and seemed to eat up all of Sue's income and more on various projects and schemes. To make things worse, he verbally abused her. Finally, Sue divorced him, but that didn't solve the problems. He would call her on the phone and continue to abuse her, blaming her for everything wrong in his life. When he took their 4-year-old daughter for visitation, he would put Sue down in front of the daughter and the daughter would get upset. Sue contemplated asking the court to take away visitation rights. But she wondered if that was in the child's best interest, or if she was just being vindictive.

Mark
When Mark and Carla first talked about getting divorced, they agreed that they would "keep it clean" so that they could still be friends when it was over. However, when Mark took the initiative and filed, Carla's reaction was not at all in line with how Mark saw their understanding. Mark offered to let her have the house, nearly all of its furnishings and $100 per month spousal support for a year. Carla refused this offer (which Mark had thought was quite generous), and asked, in addition, for $200 a month spousal support for two years, and a share in Mark's pension. Mark was furious with what he considered to be Carla's greed. He called her directly on the phone and told her if she didn't accept the offer, he would take it to court and ask that they just split everything down the middle (which would amount to considerably less than his original offer).

Carla accused him of bullying her. When Mark hung up he decided it was "No more Mr. Nice Guy"! He would go for everything he could.

The issues raised in these stories are not clear-cut, and they would become less so if we knew both sides. The point here is to see how conflict, begun in the marriage and intensified in divorce proceedings, can be carried on after the divorce. How do we deal with this conflict and anger?

Anger is a normal response to divorce
The first thing we need to do is to accept our anger as okay and normal in the context of divorce. Many people talk about an "amicable" divorce, but few achieve such a thing. The loss of a family—with all the dreams that go with it—is too costly for us to simply smile and wave good-bye to.

Some people feel it is wrong or unchristian to get angry. But that is not what Scripture says about anger. Jesus showed anger in the temple (Matt. 21:12–13), and the apostle Paul writes in his letter to the Ephesians (4:26) that it is okay to be angry, as long as we do not let anger lead us to sinful behavior.

While anger is normal, we do need to recognize that the way we express anger can be either helpful or destructive. It is destructive if we seek to destroy or "get back at" the person who has hurt us. We may feel justified (in exacting an eye for an eye or a tooth for a tooth), but the reality is that we hurt ourselves the most. We nurture all the feelings of hurt and bitterness in a way that keeps us in a turmoil and endangers our health.

We can express or relieve our anger in nondestructive ways such as writing out our feelings, talking with a friend, or engaging in physical exercise. There also may be times when you need to express your anger directly to your ex-spouse. At these times it is best to use the formula, "I am angry because ..." (state clearly the situation to which you have reacted with anger) and "I want ..." (state what you want to see happen). Stay away from blaming. (e.g."It's all your fault for making me feel this way!") Stay away from name-calling (e.g. "I feel angry because you are being a jerk and I want you to stop!").

We also need to determine whether an action we are contemplating is vindictive or necessary in light of the situation. In the stories above, should Sue seek to deny her ex-husband visitation rights? What about Ken agreeing to more spousal support? In such situations, it is often good to get advice from a neutral party like a counselor or minister.

Regardless of the situation, we have to learn to forgive our ex-spouse. We must do so not so much for their sakes, as for our own. We are seeking to nurture the growth of our new life. Every old, unforgiven hurt is a weed that can choke out that new life. Only by gently but vigilantly removing those weeds can the new life grow.

The Continuing Conflict

 ICE-BREAKER / Groups of 4 to 6 / 15 Minutes

Adolescence is a period of transition, a time when a child gradually becomes a man or woman. That requires two things: the child must take more and more control of their life and the parent must exercise less and less control over the child. Therein lies lots of opportunity for conflict!

1. When you were a teenager, what was the most memorable conflict you had with your parents? What did you do to resolve this conflict?

2. In your normal style of handling conflict, which are you more like?
    ❏ an ostrich—I hide my head in the sand.
    ❏ the neighborhood bulldog—I challenge anyone who comes near my territory.
    ❏ a house dog—I timidly slouch away, then chew up the couch when no one's looking.
    ❏ a hawk—I fly above it all and pick my targets.
    ❏ a fox—I use my brains to win.
    ❏ a wolf—I am ferocious when cornered.
    ❏ a dolphin—I can fight if necessary, but would rather swim away.
    ❏ other:_____

RESPOND TO THE VIDEO / Same Groups / 30 Minutes

1. What did your parents teach you about getting angry?

2. What nondestructive means of expressing anger have you found most helpful?

3. What physical ailments (including loss of sleep) have you suffered in the past few months? To what degree do you think this might be your body's reaction to how you are handling conflict?

4. Comparing acts of hate and vindication to weeds, how would you describe the ground around you right now?
    ❏ The weeds are completely choking me out.
    ❏ The weeds are still there, but I'm thinning them out one by one.
    ❏ New "seedlings" are popping up where the weeds used to be, but they're easier to pull up now.
    ❏ I'm ready to use "Weed-B-Gone"!
    ❏ The ground is clear and cultivated and I'm reaching for the sun!

5. Following the suggested formula, complete this sentence, "At this time in regard to my (former) marriage, I feel angry because_____ and I want_____."

Jesus was never married or divorced, but he knew what it's like to be despised and rejected. Everywhere he went, he faced criticism, ridicule and devious plots to lure him into saying or doing something that could be used against him in court. In this passage, Jesus prepared his followers for the way they must respond when they are attacked in similar ways. He says they are not to retaliate when they are attacked. They are not to be vindictive in their attitude toward their accuser. Instead they are to love, do good to, bless and pray for their enemies. At the heart of his teaching is the Golden Rule, "Do to others as you would have them do to you" (Luke 6:31).

Loving your enemies does not mean bowing to your enemy's every demand. The way Jesus stands up to the "charges" of the Pharisees makes it clear he does not expect us to simply lie down and be crushed by evil. The point he is making is that our attitude must be love; that is, we must seek the highest good of everyone—including our enemy. We are not to expect anything from our enemy in return, but we will be rewarded greatly by God himself.

ICE-BREAKER FOR TWO-SESSION OPTION
If you are doing the Bible Study as a separate session, start off this session by dividing the class into small groups of 4 to 6 and answering these questions. Photocopy and give this to the group.

Nearly everyone has a special prescription for treating a fever or cold or other physical sickness. But what about your spiritual and emotional ailments? What do you do to overcome them and restore your health?

1. If your inner spiritual state during this past week could be measured with a thermometer, what would have been your temperature?
    ❐ 98.6 degrees—normal, healthy, full of vitality
    ❐ 97.5 degrees—turning cold in the midst of stress and demands
    ❐ 99.9 degrees—Probably no one noticed, but I've been a little out of sorts.
    ❐ 102 degrees—Things have definitely been heating up inside me.
    ❐ 106 degrees—The stress is burning my brain, everything is hazy, and I'm not sure how I made it this far!

2. In the midst of what is happening inside you, what has been your favorite "fever reducer" this past week?
    ❐ a friend or friends who have listened
    ❐ my prayer and devotional time
    ❐ support from this group
    ❐ my kids or extended family
    ❐ my time alone
    ❐ watching TV and losing myself in the misery of others

SESSION TWO BIBLE STUDY

📖 27"But I tell you who hear me: Love your enemies, do good to those who hate you, 28bless those who curse you, pray for those who mistreat you. 29If someone strikes you on one cheek, turn to him the other also. If someone takes your cloak, do not stop him from taking your tunic. 30Give to everyone who asks you, and if anyone takes what belongs to you, do not demand it back. 31Do to others as you would have them do to you.

32"If you love those who love you, what credit is that to you? Even 'sinners' love those who love them. 33And if you do good to those who are good to you, what credit is that to you? Even 'sinners' do that. 34And if you lend to those from whom you expect repayment, what credit is that to you? Even 'sinners' lend to 'sinners,' expecting to be repaid in full. 35But love your enemies, do good to them, and lend to them without expecting to get anything back. Then your reward will be great, and you will be sons of the Most High, because he is kind to the ungrateful and wicked. 36Be merciful, just as your Father is merciful."

Luke 6:27–36

1. When it comes to loving and forgiving your ex-spouse, where are you right now?

-5	-4	-3	-2	-1	0	1	2	3	4	5
hating		feeling anger			numb		learning to forgive			forgiving

2. In terms of responding to your ex-spouse, which of the following is the most difficult thing for you to do?
   ❏ blessing my ex-spouse when he/she curses me
   ❏ not retaliating when he/she verbally strikes me
   ❏ not stopping him/her from taking some things that belonged to us both
   ❏ praying for him/her
   ❏ actively trying to do something positive for him/her
   ❏ not expecting anything in return for my kindness

3. In seeking to forgive your ex-spouse, what is the biggest barrier you have to overcome?
   ❏ feeling sorry for myself
   ❏ bad memories which keep returning to my mind
   ❏ the anger building up inside of me
   ❏ the need to admit I am part of the problem
   ❏ fear of the future (I'd rather dwell on the past!)
   ❏ fear of being hurt again
   ❏ other:_____

4. God promises that he will reward people who love their enemies without expecting anything in return. What would it mean to you if you really believed that God himself would reward you every time you responded to your ex-spouse in love instead of in retaliation?

Luke 6:27–36

6:27 *Love.* The Jews only regarded fellow Jews as their neighbors, but Jesus makes it clear that there is no one to whom love is not owed. The word used for love is *agape*. This type of love is not a matter of how you feel, but what you do. *Agape* love is benevolent action done for another without the expectation of reward. It is shown by actively seeking the good of those who hate, blessing those who curse, praying for those who would mistreat, and willingly giving to those who would rob.

6:29–30 These examples are not meant to be applied literally as a personal or social philosophy (which would allow evildoers free reign to exercise their whims), but are hyperbolic examples of the principles of nonretaliation, generosity, and nonpossessiveness which are to shape the life of the Christian.

6:29 *cloak.* An outer robe made of wool and used as a blanket at night.

tunic. The close fitting under-robe. Jesus uses the humorous picture of a robber being encouraged to take even more than he intended to steal in order to emphasize the spirit of giving that ought to characterize his followers (v. 30).

6:31 The "Golden Rule" sums up what the righteousness of the disciples is to look like in terms of human relationships. The negative form of this rule ("Do not do to others what you do not want them to do to you") is found in Chinese, Jewish, Hindu, Buddhist, Greek and Roman literature. Jesus, however, alters this statement in a highly significant way. Whereas the negative rule was fulfilled by simply not bothering others, the positive rule requires the active pursuit of love toward others.

6:32–36 This section underscores the fact that such acts of love are to transcend the normal boundaries of friendship. While even "sinners" show courtesy to friends, only those who reflect God's image can imitate his type of selfless love.

6:35 *reward.* This is the promise mentioned in Luke 6:20–22.

sons of the Most High. A son is one who reflects the character of the father. While the Jews assumed their relationship with God was based on their physical descent from Abraham, Jesus emphasizes that a lifestyle of love is the true mark of a child of God.

SESSION

3

Children: The Wounded Innocent

OBJECTIVES

To help us see how single parents can help their children, while at the same time caring for their own needs.

To heighten our awareness of how we can share our pain with other family members, including children.

To consider how God worked in the lives of a single mother and her son in the Old Testament.

THREE-PART AGENDA

ICE-BREAKER	**VIDEO / RESPONSE**	**BIBLE STUDY**
15 Minutes	45 Minutes	30–45 Minutes

OPTION: If you only have 60 minutes, divide this session into two sessions, with the Bible Study section for your next time together.

ICE-BREAKER

Pass out the Handout for this session and divide the class into groups of 4 to 6 to get acquainted before showing the video. Photocopy pages 26 and 28 as needed so that each person has their own Handout.

Of course there's no such thing as a perfect home or family. But taking a look back can help us see not only what was lacking in our childhood, but also what was good about it!

1. Describe the home you lived in when you were 7 years old. What was your favorite place in that home?

2. What were your parents like when you were growing up and how would you describe their marriage?

3. What did you have as a child which you would like to pass on to your children or any children you may influence?
   - ❏ a sense of security
   - ❏ knowledge of being loved
   - ❏ belief in a safe world
   - ❏ belief in the goodness of people
   - ❏ belief in God
   - ❏ self-confidence
   - ❏ an ability to use fantasy and imagination
   - ❏ self-respect

Approximately 57 percent of all divorces today involve children. That means a lot of young lives are affected when marriages break up. By the end of the 1980s about 45 percent of all children in the U.S. had witnessed the divorce of their parents.[3] As parents of these children, we must not only deal with our own period of mourning, but we must deal with the grief of our children as well.

While a substantial number of divorced people do not have children, their divorce may still have an effect on other children—nephews, nieces and other children with whom they were close—as well as on adult members of their ex-spouse's family.

Caring for ourselves and our children

One issue we frequently wrestle with as parents is how we can care for our children when it seems at times to be all we can do to care for ourselves. There are two sides to this issue:

- **To care for our children, we must care for ourselves.** Divorce therapist Bruce Fisher says, "If you are a parent who is embarking on the Rebuilding journey, my suggestion is that you learn to take care of yourself and the adjustment process that you need. You will find that your children will tend to adjust more easily as a result."[4] Note the reason this is true is that what scares children most is to be in a chaotic, uncontrolled environment. Since parents are the most important fixture in a child's life, it is vital that we regain a sense of control and mastery of our lives.

- **Sometimes caring for a child is also caring for ourselves.** What children need most is encouragement to express their feelings about what has happened, and that's what we need, too. If our children are sad and miss having their family together, we can tell them that we are sad, too, and miss being together as a family. That sometimes may even mean crying together. Children need to know that "big" boys and girls can cry, and it's even good for them to cry sometimes.

Sharing must be honest, but not destructive

Our sharing with children must be honest without burdening them with unneeded, emotionally charged details. The fact that "Daddy has found another woman he wants to be with" needs to be shared and dealt with emotionally. But details of that new relationship do not need to be shared. In such sharing children should not be used as our way of getting back at an "errant" former spouse, by turning the children against him or her. If we want our children to adjust, we can best do that by assuring them that our ex-spouse still loves them, and by pointing out some positive qualities in their other parent, with which the children can identify. To make children feel bad about a parent only makes them feel bad about themselves.

We should, however, be honest with children. Nothing can hurt a child more than to expect something from a parent and not receive it. Take, for example, the following story:

When Jessica was a little girl, her father frequently promised to visit her and then failed to follow through. It tore her mother's heart to watch little Jessica sitting out front of their home waiting for the visit that never came, and then seeing the tears well up in her eyes. At some point Jessica's mother had to honestly say, "Your Daddy means well, but he doesn't always do what he says he will do. Let's try not to count on his visit until we see him."

It is also helpful if we can share our feelings with adult members of the ex-spouse's family. We tend to forget that parents of divorcing children (or adult children of divorcing parents) also go through a grief process. Someone they thought of as part of the family is being taken away from them. Some former in-laws maintain good relationships after the divorce, but often the relationship is strained. The key is being honest and not being defensive.

Overcoming worries about a "broken home"

Many divorcing parents worry about how the marital breakup will affect their children in the long run. We have all heard people brush off a child's behavior problems by saying, "She comes from a 'broken' home." Maybe, previous to our divorce, we even said that ourselves. Now we wonder if our children have a chance of turning out all right.

There is no guarantee that any child will grow up well, and divorce does not necessarily cause permanent problems in children. (What does cause problems is prolonged, unresolved hostilities.) It is true that divorce does cause strain on children, and we should expect some behavior problems, at least initially. But these problems are nothing that cannot be taken care of with a combination of love and firmness. In other words, such problems are fixable.

Jim Smoke writes:

"I resent the use of the term 'a broken home' to describe a divorce. A broken home seems to convey to me the idea that it is permanently destroyed and the people who have lived there are beyond repair. ... A better attitude and response would be to acknowledge that your home environment was dented, dinged, bent or bruised. These terms admit damage, but do not preclude repair."[5]

A family is a system, much like a body is a system. As illness anywhere in the body disrupts the whole body, a divorce in a family system disrupts the whole system for a while. The body eventually adjusts and repairs its damaged parts, and the family can also—whether parents of divorcing children, adult children of divorcing parents, or even the youngest, most vulnerable child. We need to remember that just as disruption affects us all, so does healthy growth. If we make choices that will lead to our health and growth, we can encourage the same kinds of choices in our children and loved ones.

Children: The Wounded Innocent

 ICE-BREAKER / Groups of 4 to 6 / 15 Minutes

Of course there's no such thing as a perfect home or family. But taking a look back can help us see not only what was lacking in our childhood, but also what was good about it!

1. Describe the home you lived in when you were 7 years old. What was your favorite place in that home?

2. What were your parents like when you were growing up and how would you describe their marriage?

3. What did you have as a child which you would like to pass on to your children or any children you may influence?

   ❏ a sense of security   ❏ knowledge of being loved
   ❏ belief in a safe world   ❏ belief in the goodness of people
   ❏ belief in God   ❏ self-confidence
   ❏ an ability to use fantasy and imagination
   ❏ self-respect

 RESPOND TO THE VIDEO / Same Groups / 30 Minutes

1. What experience did you have, before your own divorce, with children of "broken homes"? How has your perspective changed? How do you react to the term "broken home"?

2. If you were to do a "systems check" on your extended family (like a mechanic might do on a car), what parts of your family system do you think you'd find had been thrown most out of kilter by your divorce? (Check all that apply.)

   ❏ my relationship to my children   ❏ my relationship to my parents
   ❏ my relationship to brothers and sisters   ❏ other:_____
   ❏ my ex-spouse's relationship to our children
   ❏ my children's behavior and emotional stability
   ❏ my relationship to former in-laws

3. If you had your child (or loved one most affected by your divorce) in front of you right now, what would be the main message you would want to convey to them? Is there anything that prevents you from sharing that message when you next see this person?

4. What healthy growth do you see in yourself that will eventually result in good things for your child or the loved one you are most concerned about?

Often a divorce has an immediate effect on a child's behavior, but sometimes the reaction is delayed. We may feel our family has survived the main crisis of the divorce itself, and is holding up remarkably well in the aftermath. Then we face an unexpected crisis and suddenly our hope for security is severely threatened.

The Bible tells a story about a single mother who was struggling to provide for herself and her son. Though she was a widow (and not divorced), her story shows how life for single parents can go from bad to better to very bad! The woman's name is never mentioned, but she is known as the widow at Zarephath, a woman God chose to provide for his prophet Elijah during a time of drought. Elijah meets her near the town gate where she is collecting sticks to make a fire to cook one last meal for herself and her son before they die (1 Kings 17:12). Elijah asks her to give him some water and bread, and prophesies that God will miraculously restore the jar of flour and the jug of oil every time she uses it. She does what Elijah asks and allows him to live in an attic room in her house. The prophecy proves true: the widow's flour and oil miraculously never runs out! Life goes very well for the prophet, the widow and her son—until tragedy once again comes upon the widow.

ICE-BREAKER FOR TWO-SESSION OPTION
If you are doing the Bible Study as a separate session, start off this session by dividing the class into small groups of 4 to 6 and answering these questions. Photocopy and give this to the group.

A vacation can be memorable in many ways! A week in a cabin on the beach is great, unless a storm front sits off the coast for seven straight days! On the other hand, beautiful weather and nice accommodations can make for a vacation worth remembering for a long time!

1. Describe your past week as if it were a vacation.
   - ❏ a Caribbean cruise—smooth sailing all the way
   - ❏ a backpacking trip—carrying some burdens, but experiencing some great things
   - ❏ a Safari—a lot of frightening stuff, but still an adventure
   - ❏ a day at the beach—until I got hit by a tidal wave
   - ❏ a camping trip in the rain—I want to go where it's safe and warm!
   - ❏ a car trip across the back roads of America—I keep getting lost, but I've got all the time in the world!
   - ❏ a canoe trip, with my canoe overturned—I've lost everything, so how can I go on?
   - ❏ other:_____

2. If you were writing home from this trip to convince everyone you were having a good time, what event would you point to as the highlight of your trip?

SESSION THREE BIBLE STUDY

[17]Some time later the son of the woman who owned the house became ill. He grew worse and worse, and finally stopped breathing. [18]She said to Elijah, "What do you have against me, man of God? Did you come to remind me of my sin and kill my son?"

[19]"Give me your son," Elijah replied. He took him from her arms, carried him to the upper room where he was staying, and laid him on his bed. [20]Then he cried out to the LORD, "O LORD my God, have you brought tragedy also upon this widow I am staying with, by causing her son to die?" [21]Then he stretched himself out on the boy three times and cried to the LORD, "O LORD my God, let this boy's life return to him!"

[22]The LORD heard Elijah's cry, and the boy's life returned to him, and he lived. [23]Elijah picked up the child and carried him down from the room into the house. He gave him to his mother and said, "Look, your son is alive!"

[24]Then the woman said to Elijah, "Now I know that you are a man of God and that the word of the LORD from your mouth is the truth."

1 Kings 17:17–24

1. Judging by her comments to Elijah, what do you think the widow was feeling most strongly when her son stopped breathing? How was she changed after God brought him back to life?

2. The widow of Zarephath and her son were down to their last meal when Elijah came into their lives. When, since your divorce or time of marital stress, have you—and your child(ren)—reached the end of your rope?

3. God used some of the widow's own resources—a jar of flour and a jug of oil—to provide for her and her son. What are some resources you have that God may want to use to strengthen you and your child(ren)?

   ❐ some friends I have overlooked   ❐ prayer and devotional time
   ❐ the church   ❐ my extended family
   ❐ an inner strength I didn't know I had   ❐ a community helping agency
   ❐ Scripture   ❐ an educational opportunity
   ❐ professional counseling   ❐ a new love relationship

4. What keeps you from believing that your child(ren) will turn out all right?
   ❐ My faith is weak.
   ❐ I used up my last flour and oil a long time ago.
   ❐ I'm not willing to let my child(ren) go.
   ❐ I haven't seen any miracles yet.
   ❐ I lack confidence in my child(ren).
   ❐ The spark of life inside my child(ren) is almost out.
   ❐ I'm getting exactly what I deserve; I can't expect more than that.
   ❐ I'm too much of a realist to have hope.

1 Kings 17:17–24

17:17–24 Prior to this story, Elijah had prophesied to King Ahab that there would be a drought over the next few years until Elijah spoke another word of prophecy. God warned Elijah to flee for his life to the east of the Jordan River. There he was fed daily by ravens who brought him bread and meat, and he drank from a brook. When the brook dried up (due to the drought), the Lord told the prophet to go to the town of Zarephath, where a widow had been commanded to provide him with food and shelter. Elijah meets the widow at the gate, where she is picking up sticks to cook her last meal for herself and her son. Elijah asks her for some bread and prophesies that God will supply her needs by making it so that her jar of flour and jug of oil will not run out. She obeys, and allows Elijah to live in an upper room. Life goes well for the woman, her son and Elijah, until one day the child becomes ill.

17:17 *the woman.* The widow with whom Elijah lived. The Bible does not give her name.

owned the house. Some commentators suggest that the woman may have run a boarding house or temporary refuge for travelers.

17:18 *Elijah.* Elijah means "the Lord is my God."

remind me of my sin. The woman assumes the death of her son is a punishment from God for her past sins. The same attitude is reflected in the NT, when Peter (Luke 5:8) says to Jesus, "Go away from me, Lord; I am a sinful man!" The same tendency is present in many divorced persons who assume blame for problems their children are having.

17:19–20 Elijah takes the boy to this own room and prays for healing.

O Lord my God, have you brought tragedy. Elijah's approach to God reflects both respect for who God is and confidence that God can handle Elijah's questions and strong emotions.

17:21 *he stretched himself out on the boy three times.* Elijah "acts out" his intentions for the boy, as if to say, "Let this lifeless body be as my lively body" (DeVries). Similar healings take place elsewhere in the Bible: Elisha, successor of Elijah, heals a child (2 Kings 4:34) and the apostle Paul heals a man who fell out a window (Acts 20:10).

17:22 God answers the prayers of Elijah and the boy is restored to life.

17:23–24 The restoration of the boy's life has two important messages for the widow: that she was wrong to assume her son's death was a punishment for hidden sin in her life; and that Elijah was indeed a man of God and his words were true.

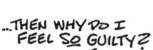

4

Opening Ourselves to Grace

OBJECTIVES

To share the feelings of failure which often accompany divorce.

To discover together the forgiveness which God in his grace wants us to know.

To look at a Bible story of divine forgiveness and see what it says to us.

THREE-PART AGENDA

| ICE-BREAKER | VIDEO / RESPONSE | BIBLE STUDY |
| 15 Minutes | 45 Minutes | 30–45 Minutes |

OPTION: If you only have 60 minutes, divide this session into two sessions, with the Bible Study section for your next time together.

ICE-BREAKER

Pass out the Handout for this session and divide the class into groups of 4 to 6 to get acquainted before showing the video. Photocopy pages 34 and 36 as needed so that each person has their own Handout.

Caught Red-handed! There may be no more humiliating experience than that of being found out! Sometimes such experiences can stick with us for a lifetime.

1. When you were 9 years old, what were you most likely to be guilty of?
   ❏ shoplifting   ❏ telling on my friends or siblings
   ❏ smoking   ❏ not getting my schoolwork done
   ❏ playing "doctor"   ❏ other:_____
   ❏ lying to my parents
   ❏ taking money from my parents' dresser

2. If you did something wrong at that age, how would your parents generally find out?
   ❏ I would confess.   ❏ I had a guilty look on my face.
   ❏ I was a lousy liar.   ❏ Someone would tell on me.
   ❏ I don't know—they just knew!
   ❏ They didn't—in fact, they still haven't!
   ❏ I did a poor job of concealing evidence (smoke on my breath!).

We have already seen how hard it is to forgive an ex-spouse. But for many of us there is something even more difficult—forgiving ourselves! It is hard to forgive ourselves because we often feel we have failed so many people, and our sense of guilt goes right to the core of who we are.

However, we can become free of the weight of this guilt if we are willing to take the necessary steps. In fact, if we are feeling guilty over our role in the breakup of our marriage, we have already made significant progress on the road to finding forgiveness and release from shame!

Why we need forgiveness

Divorce often means failure on three fronts: we have failed ourselves, other people and God.

- **We have failed ourselves.** We have fallen short of our dream of a good marriage and a happy home. Certainly we know—and our friends tell us—that our divorce was not all our fault. However, many of us live at an emotional level according to the principle, "If in doubt, it probably is my fault!" That conclusion is flawed, since it takes two people to make a marriage and two people to break one. Nevertheless, many of us are all too willing to accept the entire blame. Singles minister Jim Smoke writes, "The finest court in the land could not examine all the intricacies that combined to cause a marriage to fail. Few counselors are skilled enough to assess who or what caused the marriage to disintegrate. Lacking a pronouncement of some form that would place the blame, many people who go through divorce take the blame upon themselves."[6]

- **We have failed others.** We feel we have failed our children because we didn't provide a stable home. Some of us feel we have failed our parents by not living up to the ideals they taught us. Some even feel we have failed our former spouse. Take, for instance, Ted. He talked of how shocked he was when his wife of 14 years filed for divorce:

  "I felt numb inside. I kept replaying different scenes from the past few months over and over in my mind. Just six months ago she had written me a note saying how glad she was that I was her best friend and husband. What had gone wrong? What was it that I couldn't see? Where had I not listened to her? These questions plagued me for months as I compiled an ever-growing list of how I had let her down."

- **We have failed God.** The Bible clearly speaks against divorce. Many of us heard these words at our wedding: "Therefore what God has joined together, let man not separate" (Matt. 19:6). In Matthew 5:32 Jesus warns, "But I tell you that anyone who divorces his wife, except for marital unfaithfulness, causes her to become an adulteress, and anyone who marries the divorced woman commits adultery."

The way we respond to such verses depends in part on whether we were the initiator of our divorce. Many divorced people, however, cannot hear such verses without heightened feelings of failure and even despair. Church members often aggravate such feelings by saying things we perceive as judgmental ("Well, my Harry and I have troubles, too, but we believe we should work at our marriage instead of taking the easy way out!"). Such statements—and our perceptions of them—lead many of us to avoid church altogether.

Separating true guilt from false guilt

We must remember that while God uses guilt to convict us of sin, it is not true that every guilty feeling comes from God. We must distinguish between appropriate guilt and neurotic guilt.

- **Neurotic guilt**—also known as false guilt or shame—condemns and punishes us for things that we cannot change, cannot attain or are not responsible for. It bruises our self-esteem and leaves us with an overwhelming sense that we are "no good." Sue kept blaming herself after her husband, without warning, left her for another woman. "I could have been a better wife," she kept saying. The fact is that every husband and wife who ever lived could have been a better spouse. It is unrealistic to expect that you must suffer in guilt forever because of your divorce. False guilt does not require repentance on our part because the problem is not our performance, but our unrealistic expectations. We had attempted to live up to impossible standards which God himself did not demand of us.

- **Appropriate guilt**—or healthy guilt—is like pain. Just as God allows pain to warn us of damage to our bodies, he gave us guilt to warn us when something may be spiritually wrong and when damage to our spirit has occurred.

When we feel guilty, we need to open our hearts to God and ask his forgiveness. This is what grace is all about. Grace is being accepted by God on the basis of his mercy rather than our performance. It is a free gift and leads to a fresh start for those who accept it.

God does not want us to be chained by our past failures. Christ, in dying on the cross, took our sins upon himself and paid the penalty for our sin (true guilt). The result for us is freedom from guilt and punishment. In light of this, to cling to feelings of guilt and failure is to reject the grace of God.

- If we continue to punish ourselves, we are undoing Christ's payment for our sins.
- If we let ourselves be burdened by our feelings of failure, we are rejecting the very freedom Christ came to bring.
- In the end, the way we respond to grace will determine whether we can be released from our feelings of guilt. Because of God's forgiveness, we have the opportunity for a fresh start in life!

Opening Ourselves to Grace

 ICE-BREAKER / Groups of 4 to 6 / 15 Minutes

Caught Red-handed! There may be no more humiliating experience than that of being found out! Sometimes such experiences can stick with us for a lifetime.

1. When you were 9 years old, what were you most likely to be guilty of?
   - ❒ shoplifting
   - ❒ smoking
   - ❒ playing "doctor"
   - ❒ taking money from my parents' dresser
   - ❒ telling on my friends or siblings
   - ❒ not getting my schoolwork done
   - ❒ lying to my parents
   - ❒ other:_____

2. If you did something wrong at that age, how would your parents generally find out?
   - ❒ They didn't—in fact, they still haven't!
   - ❒ I was a lousy liar.
   - ❒ I don't know—they just knew!
   - ❒ I did a poor job of concealing evidence (smoke on my breath!).
   - ❒ I had a guilty look on my face.
   - ❒ Someone would tell on me.
   - ❒ I would confess.

🖵 **RESPOND TO THE VIDEO** / Same Groups / 30 Minutes

1. What is your immediate reaction to all of these thoughts about guilt, shame, the need for forgiveness and the role of Jesus Christ in our forgiveness?
   - ❒ It sounds like something I need to think through.
   - ❒ I've done a lot of thinking already on this issue.
   - ❒ I'd rather not think about it.
   - ❒ It makes me angry.
   - ❒ I'd prefer to keep Jesus out of this.
   - ❒ I'm not sure I'm ready to work on forgiving myself.

2. There is guilt that is false or neurotic, and there is guilt that is appropriate and comes from God. From your experience, how can a person determine which kind of guilt they are feeling?

3. If feelings of failure form a prison around us, where are you right now?
   - ❒ in a maximum security cell and it looks like a life sentence
   - ❒ in a minimum security prison, but it's not so bad
   - ❒ like a trustee—sometimes in prison, sometimes away from it
   - ❒ I'm planning a jail break!
   - ❒ I've been paroled!

4. To break free from your prison of feelings of failure, what do you most need to do?

Jesus spent very little time with people who outwardly seemed to "have it all together." Normally he was with poor, working people like fishermen or unpopular people like tax collectors—people who knew they were struggling sinners.

The following story is one of the rare instances when Jesus attended a social occasion at the home of a religious leader. The host, whose name was Simon, was a member of the Pharisees—a powerful Jewish sect who rigidly held to religious laws and codes of conduct and typically looked down on people who didn't. Imagine the charged atmosphere in the room as an uninvited guest—most likely a prostitute—does something which changes the whole flavor of the evening, from theological debate to an emotional exchange on the grace of God. The "sinful woman" had something in common with a divorced person: She had a heightened awareness of failure because her failure was public knowledge. But Jesus saw that awareness on her part as a step in the right direction—the direction of finding forgiveness and wholeness.

> ## ICE-BREAKER FOR TWO-SESSION OPTION
> *If you are doing the Bible Study as a separate session, start off this session by dividing the class into small groups of 4 to 6 and answering these questions. Photocopy and give this to the group.*

On the Floor of the Stock Market. Few things move faster—or have more ups and downs—than the stock market, though sometimes our lives almost approach that level!

1. If your life this past week were the stock market, how would you describe the week's activity?
    ❏ unchanged in active trading—a lot happening, some good, some bad
    ❏ unchanged in light trading—nothing happening
    ❏ closed slightly lower—no depression, but I may be going through a recession
    ❏ closed slightly higher—Things look a little better, but nobody would get rich off of me.
    ❏ a rally—Everything I'm investing in is paying dividends!
    ❏ a crash—If I could have, I would have "suspended trading"!
    ❏ other:_____

2. If you were a broker, advising people whether to invest in you for the coming week, would you be more "bearish" (pessimistic) or more "bullish" (optimistic)?

SESSION FOUR BIBLE STUDY

36 Now one of the Pharisees invited Jesus to have dinner with him, so he went to the Pharisee's house and reclined at the table. 37 When a woman who had lived a sinful life in that town learned that Jesus was eating at the Pharisee's house, she brought an alabaster jar of perfume, 38 and as she stood behind him at his feet weeping, she began to wet his feet with her tears. Then she wiped them with her hair, kissed them and poured perfume on them.

39 When the Pharisee who had invited him saw this, he said to himself, "If this man were a prophet, he would know who is touching him and what kind of woman she is—that she is a sinner."

40 Jesus answered him, "Simon, I have something to tell you."

"Tell me, teacher," he said.

41 "Two men owed money to a certain moneylender. One owed him five hundred denarii, and the other fifty. 42 Neither of them had the money to pay him back, so he canceled the debts of both. Now which of them will love him more?"

43 Simon replied, "I suppose the one who had the bigger debt canceled."

"You have judged correctly," Jesus said.

44 Then he turned toward the woman and said to Simon, "Do you see this woman? I came into your house. You did not give me any water for my feet, but she wet my feet with her tears and wiped them with her hair. 45 You did not give me a kiss, but this woman, from the time I entered, has not stopped kissing my feet. 46 You did not put oil on my head, but she has poured perfume on my feet. 47 Therefore, I tell you, her many sins have been forgiven— for she loved much. But he who has been forgiven little loves little."

48 Then Jesus said to her, "Your sins are forgiven."

49 The other guests began to say among themselves, "Who is this who even forgives sins?"

50 Jesus said to the woman, "Your faith has saved you; go in peace."

Luke 7:36–50

1. How would you have felt watching this woman anoint Jesus like she did in verse 38? Why do you think the woman, likely a prostitute, expressed her repentance and love like this—instead of verbally?

2. When in your life have you (like this woman) felt like an outsider who didn't belong?

3. What person or group has played the part of Simon the Pharisee in your life, judging and condemning you, since your divorce or marital trouble?
   - ❐ my parents
   - ❐ the church
   - ❐ my ex-spouse
   - ❐ my former in-laws
   - ❐ my former friends
   - ❐ myself
   - ❐ my children
   - ❐ other:_____

4. During your time of divorce, what person or group has helped you most to experience the love and forgiveness of God, as shown by Jesus in this story?

Luke 7:36–50

7:36 *one of the Pharisees.* "The fact that (Jesus) was especially inter-
ested in despised people did not mean that he was uninterested in the
more respectable members of society" (Marshall). Why Simon (v. 40)
invited him is unclear. His lack of providing some of the common courte-
sies to his guest (vv. 44–46) indicates his opinion of Jesus probably was
not especially high. He may have even been trying to trap Jesus.

reclined at the table. People ate by reclining on their left side on low
couches arranged around a table such that their feet would be stretched
out behind them.

7:37 *a sinful life.* While not stated, most likely a life of sexual immorality—perhaps prostitution—is meant. The woman, who was certainly not
an invited guest, may simply have joined other people in Simon's court-
yard who had gathered to listen to Jesus talk.

7:38 This verse is loaded with emotion. The woman's tears show her
extreme conviction as she stood by the foot of Jesus. For a woman to
loose her hair in public was scandalous; using it to dry her tears from
Jesus' feet marked her great humility before him. Normally, a person's
head would be anointed as a sign of honor. Like John the Baptist, who felt
unworthy to undo the thongs of the Messiah's sandals (Luke 3:16), this
woman felt so unworthy that she could dare only anoint Jesus' feet.

7:39 Simon, seeing only that Jesus violated the acceptable religious and
social code by allowing such a woman to touch him like this, saw nothing of her repentance or gratitude. If he had invited Jesus to dinner with
the hope of finding fault with the rumors about his being a great prophet
of God, he was sure he had it now. Since Jesus did not draw away from
the woman, either he did not know what type of woman she was (showing he lacked a prophet's discernment), or he was not put off by her
immorality (showing he lacked a prophet's holiness).

7:40–47 Through a brief parable and interpretation, Jesus disarms
Simon's silent criticism. He reveals that he indeed does discern what is in
the hearts of people (both the woman's *and* Simon's), and that he is concerned about holiness which comes about through the forgiveness of sin.
By this parable he highlights his mission of saving those who recognize
their sin, and forces Simon (as well as the reader) to question whether he
has ever come to grips with the reality of his own sin.

7:47 Jesus is not saying that the woman is forgiven *because* she has
shown such extravagant love (just as the debt was not canceled
because of any act on the part of the creditor—v. 42), but that her love
expresses the reality of the forgiveness she has received. Jesus states
clearly in verse 50 that she was saved by faith.

SESSION

5

Fashioning a New Self

OBJECTIVES

To see how marital conflict and divorce changes the way we perceive ourselves.

To find a more solid basis on which to build our self-image.

To look at a story from the Bible to see how God can help us rebuild our view of self.

THREE-PART AGENDA

ICE-BREAKER
15 Minutes

VIDEO / RESPONSE
45 Minutes

BIBLE STUDY
30–45 Minutes

OPTION: If you only have 60 minutes, divide this session into two sessions, with the Bible Study section for your next time together.

ICE-BREAKER

Pass out the Handout for this session and divide the class into groups of 4 to 6 to get acquainted before showing the video. Photocopy pages 42 and 44 as needed so that each person has their own Handout.

Childhood Dreams and Heroes. Our childhood heroes and childhood dreams often give us more than a glimpse of what we had hoped to be. Often they give us an idea of what we still hope to become. How closely have you held onto your childhood fantasies? Answer the following questions to see:

1. When you were in fourth grade (ages 9–10), what person—real or fictional—did you most want to be like? What qualities in this person did you desire most for yourself?

2. When you were in fourth grade, what did you dream about becoming and doing when you grew up?

3. Who did you share your dreams with?
    ❒ my parents   ❒ my brother or sister
    ❒ a grandparent   ❒ a teacher
    ❒ my best friend, _____ ❒ other:_____
    ❒ nobody—They would have laughed!

39

In the book, *Alice's Adventures in Wonderland,* the Caterpillar asks Alice, "Who are you?" Her answer is intriguing: "I—I hardly know, Sir, just at present ... at least I know who I was when I got up this morning, but I think I must have changed several times since then." Alice's answer could also be given by many divorced people. Divorce turns our world so upside down that we end up losing touch with our own identity.

This loss of identity happens with both sexes, but can be particularly acute in women. Most men are more likely to find their identity in their profession, while most women are more relationship-oriented and find their identity in their family relationships, primarily their marriage. Whether a woman's view of marriage was realistic doesn't necessarily take away the pain of the loss of a husband. Consider what each of these three women felt they had lost:

- **Prince**—Jackie related her loss of identity to one of our popular children's stories: "I had real difficulties pulling myself out of feeling as if I was 'nothing' without a man. I grew up in the Cinderella-complex age where a man was supposed to make you happy, care for you, make you complete, and so on. My former spouse nurtured that idea."[7]

- **Protector**—Carmen similarly commented, "I went from being my daddy's little girl to being my husband's little girl. Now that we are divorced, I don't know who I am on my own."

- **Mirror**—After Connie's divorce, she wrote, "I didn't just lose a husband, I lost my way of evaluating myself. He was my mirror. Now I don't know how I look anymore."[8]

While this loss of identity seems to be acute for women, it is often a problem for men too. Brett reported that years after his divorce he would look at pictures of himself from his previous marriage and wonder if he was the same person at all as the person pictured. He joked about things that happened then as experiences "from a previous life."

Self-worth tied to personal identity

Part of this loss of identity is a loss of our self-worth. Our identity is the foundation upon which we build a sense of who we are and what we do. When our identity is gone, our sense of worth goes with it. People who are recently separated have an extremely low sense of self-worth. Bruce Fisher, a counselor who has administered the *Tennessee Self-Concept Scale* (a measure of people's feelings of self-worth) to many groups of people, writes in regard to the test scores of recently separated people, "It would be hard to find another group of people whose average score was as low as theirs."[9]

As divorced people, then, we may have to start at ground level in regard to our sense of identity and worth. That can be frightening because we have so little to hang on to. But it can also be an exciting adventure. We have cleared the ground and we are starting to rebuild! If we build well, we can structure our new self-concept on a much stronger foundation than the old one. No longer will our view of who we are rest on whom we happen to be married to, or our attempts to play out childhood fairy tales, or the sometimes distorted mirror of another person's opinion. Perhaps now our view of self can be built upon something more certain—the gifts and qualities God has created in us.

Building steps for a new self

Building a new sense of self, like building a house or refashioning a work of art, involves several important steps. In our refashioning of ourself, our architect is God, and we need to be aware that God is ready and eager to be our partner in the building process. Dennis and Matthew Linn, in their book, *Healing of Memories,* compare this step to the refashioning of a famous work of art. They write:

> When a fanatic dealt several damaging blows to Michelangelo's Pieta, the world was horrified. It surprised no one when the world's best artists assembled to refashion the disfigured masterpiece.

> When sculptors arrived in Italy, they didn't begin repairing the marred face immediately. Rather they spent months looking at the Pieta, touching the flowing lines, appreciating the way each part expressed suffering yet ecstacy. Some spent months studying a single part such as the hand until finally the sculptors began to see more and more with the eyes of Michelangelo and to touch and feel as the master artist would have done. When the sculptors finally began repairing the face, the strokes belonged almost as much to Michelangelo as to themselves.

> Not Michelangelo's but rather God's sculpturing hand fashioned us from soil-dust into a masterpiece which surpassed even the Pieta (Gen. 2:7). It should not surprise us that God constantly refashions us—that as soon as we disfigure ourselves, He's already sculpting the pieces back together.[10]

The refashioning of the Pieta did not happen quickly. We should not expect that fashioning our new self will happen quickly. What we are looking for is God's design, God's purpose in us. Finding this takes time and effort. We have to consult the Scriptures, which lay out his blueprint for our lives. In the last chapter we saw what God says about forgiveness and how we need to accept his grace rather than "undo" the work of Christ. The same is true for building our self-esteem. We must find out what God says about who we are by reading the Bible, talking to mature friends, reading helpful books on the subject, and through personal prayer and reflection. In the midst of all this, we must give the architect time to do his work in us.

Like most people's houses, we can never be completely finished building our self-image. There is always something to touch up here and there. But when we build well, there comes a point when we can live in and enjoy our new home. That is our goal as divorced persons.

Fashioning a New Self

 ICE-BREAKER / Groups of 4 to 6 / 15 Minutes

Childhood Dreams and Heroes. Our childhood heroes and childhood dreams often give us more than a glimpse of what we had hoped to be. Often they give us an idea of what we still hope to become. How closely have you held onto your childhood fantasies? Answer the following questions to see:

1. When you were in fourth grade (ages 9–10), what person—real or fictional—did you most want to be like? What qualities in this person did you desire most for yourself?

2. When you were in fourth grade, what did you dream about becoming and doing when you grew up?

3. Who did you share your dreams with?
   - ❏ my parents
   - ❏ a grandparent
   - ❏ my best friend, _____
   - ❏ nobody—They would have laughed!
   - ❏ my brother or sister
   - ❏ a teacher
   - ❏ other:_____

RESPOND TO THE VIDEO / Same Groups / 30 Minutes

1. From your experience, do men or do women struggle more with their loss of identity after divorce? How do they struggle differently?

2. What aspects of divorce do you believe are most destructive to a person's identity?
   - ❏ suddenly having a person missing
   - ❏ changes in daily routine and ritual
   - ❏ feeling rejected
   - ❏ being separated from one who shared my past
   - ❏ being separated from the one I used to "bounce off" ideas for decision-making
   - ❏ harsh words
   - ❏ having to move
   - ❏ feeling guilt
   - ❏ other:_____

3. How would you describe the image of the new self God is wanting to fashion within you? How is God calling you to cooperate with this building project?

4. Often we are the last to recognize any positive signs of change in our own lives. We need to help each other see the good that is happening! Go around the circle and have one person at a time listen while the others share ways they have seen this person change or grow. (Note: If you are doing this unit as one combined session, you may want to wait until after the Bible Study to come back and do this exercise.)

Ezekiel prophesied when Israel was in exile in Babylonia. It was perhaps the lowest point of their history. They were separated from their homeland and their hope of being revived as a nation was fading. During this time, Ezekiel went to an old battlefield, perhaps one where Israel had lost a battle which led to their captivity and exile. The field was full of old, dry human bones from the battle, and Ezekiel saw these as symbolic of the spirit of Israel. His vision of the bones coming to life was symbolic of Israel finding a new life and identity.

Ever since this prophecy, people who have been down-and-out have seen it as a message that with God there is always hope. This hope was especially meaningful to the slaves of America's Old South who turned the story into the spiritual song, "Dem Bones." It spoke to them of their crushed hope being revived through a new life of freedom. As you read the passage, find the images of your own spiritual death and resurrection.

ICE-BREAKER FOR TWO-SESSION OPTION
If you are doing the Bible Study as a separate session, start off this session by dividing the class into small groups of 4 to 6 and answering these questions. Photocopy and give this to the group.

How Was Your Week? Certainly, our lives have more peaks and valleys than a mountain range—especially in the shadow of a divorce. Imagine the past week was a section of the trail that goes along a mountain range.

1. What characteristic about your hike this past week stands out most in your memory?
   ❏ a beautiful vista from 10,000 feet
   ❏ the steep climb up
   ❏ the weight of my "pack"
   ❏ a refreshing swim in a mountain stream
   ❏ the steep walk down
   ❏ walking along a precipice
   ❏ the hot sun beating down on me
   ❏ the order and beauty of the stars at night
   ❏ other:_____

2. What part of your hike was a little frightening for you? What part would you like to do again?

3. What lies ahead for the next few days of your trip? How are you preparing yourself for it?

37 The hand of the LORD was upon me, and he brought me out by the Spirit of the LORD and set me in the middle of a valley; it was full of bones. ²He led me back and forth among them, and I saw a great many bones on the floor of the valley, bones that were very dry. ³He asked me, "Son of man, can these bones live?"

I said, "O Sovereign LORD, you alone know."

⁴Then he said to me, "Prophesy to these bones and say to them, 'Dry bones, hear the word of the LORD! ⁵This is what the Sovereign LORD says to these bones: I will make breath enter you, and you will come to life. ⁶I will attach tendons to you and make flesh come upon you and cover you with skin; I will put breath in you, and you will come to life. Then you will know that I am the LORD.' "

⁷So I prophesied as I was commanded. And as I was prophesying, there was a noise, a rattling sound, and the bones came together, bone to bone. ⁸I looked, and tendons and flesh appeared on them and skin covered them, but there was no breath in them.

⁹Then he said to me, "Prophesy to the breath; prophesy, son of man, and say to it, 'This is what the Sovereign LORD says: Come from the four winds, O breath, and breathe into these slain, that they may live.' " ¹⁰So I prophesied as he commanded me, and breath entered them; they came to life and stood up on their feet—a vast army.

¹¹Then he said to me: "Son of man, these bones are the whole house of Israel. They say, 'Our bones are dried up and our hope is gone; we are cut off.' ¹²Therefore prophesy and say to them: 'This is what the Sovereign LORD says: O my people, I am going to open your graves and bring you up from them; I will bring you back to the land of Israel. ¹³Then you, my people, will know that I am the LORD, when I open your graves and bring you up from them. ¹⁴I will put my Spirit in you and you will live, and I will settle you in your own land. Then you will know that I the LORD have spoken, and I have done it, declares the Lord.' "

Ezekiel 37:1–14

1. How would you have felt if God had led you to a valley of old, dry human bones?
    - ❏ spooked
    - ❏ depressed at the thought of death
    - ❏ cynical about war and human nature
    - ❏ meditative
    - ❏ bewildered
    - ❏ other:_____

2. How would you have felt after the bones came to life at your command?

3. What old perceptions of yourself—which you had before your divorce or time of marital stress—seem like old, dry bones to you right now?

4. Where are you in the process of bringing your view of yourself back to life again?

5. You are looking at the old, dry bones of your identity, and God asks you the question he asked of Ezekiel: "Can these bones live?" What is your answer? Mark your response with an *"X"* on the continuum below, and share it with your group:

_____

No way!   **With God, all things are possible.**

Ezekiel 37:1–14

37:1 *The hand of the LORD was upon me.* Ezekiel is caught up in a trance, in which his mind is made to serve God's purpose. It is not clear if what Ezekiel describes here is a dream, a vision or an actual event.

a valley ... full of bones. The valley, or plain, appears to be the same place mentioned in 3:22–23 and 8:4, near Ezekiel's home in exile at Tel-Abib. The valley, which has been a place of God's judgment upon Israel, will become the place where God triumphs over death.

37:2 Two things are emphasized about the bones: their great number and their dryness. The bones being "very dry" means that they had been dead for quite some time, making their coming to life even more incredible.

37:5 *breath.* The Hebrew word *ruah* is used three different ways in this chapter: Spirit (vv. 1,14); breath (vv. 5–6,8–10); and wind/winds (v. 9). It is the same word that lies behind the meaning of the words and spirit in John 3:8: "The wind blows wherever it pleases. You hear its sound, but you cannot tell where it comes from or where it is going. So it is with everyone born of the Spirit."

37:6 *you will come to life.* The impossible is promised: the dead will live again.

Then you will know that I am the LORD. The purpose of all miracles is the same: to make God known.

37:7–8 Ezekiel obeys the command to prophesy to the bones and sees (and hears) immediate results. But there was no breath in them. Two miracles are necessary. The recreation parallels God's two-step creation of man in Genesis 2:7: God "formed the man from the dust of the ground" and "breathed into his nostrils the breath of life."

37:11 God provides the interpretation of Ezekiel's vision. The bones represent the exiles and their view that their exile means the death of their nation.

They say. Ezekiel's vision has clearly grown out of the lament of the exiles. "Our bones are dried up and our hope is gone; we are cut off." The Israelites in exile have lost their vitality, their hope of going home and ultimately their very life.

37:12 *Therefore prophesy.* As in the vision of the dry bones, God calls Ezekiel to speak words of hope to a "hopeless" situation. God responds to the exiles' laments. He will bring them up from the grave (restore their vitality): bring them back to the land of Israel (their home); and give them back their future by putting his Spirit in them.

"...IT IS DURING DIVORCE RECOVERY THAT
WE NEED FRIENDS MORE THAN EVER...."

SESSION

6

Building a Support System

OBJECTIVES

To look at how divorce affects our friendship patterns.

To talk about ways we can develop and maintain a support system of friends even after this group ends.

To look at a story from the Bible which illustrates how friends can help us find healing.

THREE-PART AGENDA

| **ICE-BREAKER**
15 Minutes | **VIDEO / RESPONSE**
45 Minutes | **BIBLE STUDY**
30–45 Minutes |

OPTION: If you only have 60 minutes, divide this session into two sessions, with the Bible Study section for your next time together.

ICE-BREAKER

Pass out the Handout for this session and divide the class into groups of 4 to 6 to get acquainted before showing the video. Photocopy pages 50 and 52 as needed so that each person has their own Handout.

Music in My Life. Go around and let everyone explain this past week—somewhere between the two extremes—in each area of their life. If you do not know the songs, just go with the titles.

IN MY WORK THIS PAST WEEK, IT HAS BEEN ...
Some days the windshield,
some days the bug _____Everything is beautiful

ABOUT MYSELF, I'M FEELING ...
Nobody loves me but my mama,
and she might be lying, too_____Jesus loves me

ABOUT THE FUTURE, I'M FEELING ...
There's a light at the end of the tunnel;   Call me a
I hope it's not a train _____cock-eyed optimist

One of the most important long-term needs we have as we recover from divorce is a support system of people who care. This is because God made us for relationship. "It is not good for the man [or a woman] to be alone" (Gen. 2:18). Being divorced may mean being single, but it does not mean we have to be alone. We need—and should get—the advice, nurture and affection which others can give.

The support group you are now in provides that for as long as you are together, but what happens beyond that? Some friendships from this group will carry over afterward and possibly become lifelong friendships. However, it is likely that other friendships will need to be developed to maintain a fully adequate support system.

Overcoming the loss of friendships
Part of the reason why divorced persons need to develop a support system is that we have lost so many of our old friends in the process of divorce. When we were married, most of our friends were also married. Singles minister Jim Smoke describes the attitude of many singles he works with when he writes:

> "I was married—I now am single," prompts a sudden shift in lifestyle from married friends to single friends. This often occurs after building only married friendships for twenty or more years.[11]

Married persons prefer married friends in part because they share a common status and common interests. In part, too, there is the issue of jealousy—a single friend can be seen as a threat to the same sex member of a couple. And finally, some married persons simply do not know how to act around single persons—perhaps because they have never learned the skills necessary to put themselves into another person's situation.

Old friendships from a marriage can also dissipate because of the tensions involved in the divorce. Author Diane Vaughan, puts it this way: "Significant relationships are lost to both partners, as friends hear the conflicting accounts, and either align with one or the other or simply drop out of sight because they are unable to choose between the two and find it difficult to support both." The result, Vaughan says, is "they retreat, isolating the newly separated."[12]

Carl
After Carl filed for divorce he wrote a letter to three different couples whom he hadn't seen for a while. He shared his feelings about what had happened, and told how much he desired their friendship to continue. One couple invited Carl for dinner and Carl was uplifted by the empathy and friendship they showed him on that occasion. However, he never heard from the other friends. He later heard that both couples had shown support and continued friendship to his former wife. They had said that they "wanted to be friends with both, but could not," so they chose Carl's former wife because she "needed them more."

Greg

Greg's former wife had been the initiator of their divorce, and at first Greg's married friends were quite supportive. But in time Greg said he began to feel like an outsider at their home and that they treated him as a "charity case." The invitations to visit became fewer and fewer, and his once-intimate friendships became rather distant.

Gaining and maintaining new friendships

The isolation we often feel from former friends is especially painful since it is during divorce recovery that we need friends more than ever. It becomes very important that we develop the skills needed to gain and maintain new friendships. This can be particularly difficult for men, who are often less adept than women at social skills. Many men have not been raised to share their true feelings and often are so job-focused that they don't take time for friendships. Some psychologists, in fact, say that only about 10 percent of the adult men in our country have what they consider to be close friends. Whether we are a man or a woman, if we do not cultivate a support system, we miss out on what such a system can give us:

• Someone to cheer us on when we want to give up.
• Someone to help us sort out possibilities for decision-making.
• Someone to share feelings with in a therapeutic way.
• Someone to just give us a hug when we need physical reassurance.

Divorced persons have some advantages

One advantage that single people have in developing friendships is that they don't have the time obligations that go with a marriage (if there are no young children in the picture). It is also true that other divorced people are in the same boat we are, and they may be highly motivated to make connections with us.

Sometimes the experience of divorce even helps us open up and be better friends. Author Alan Loy McGinnis reports, "A woman whose marriage recently ended says her friendships have a new closeness and warmth since her divorce. 'I used to hear other people's troubles,' she said, 'but never told my own. Now I can let it all out.' The other day someone told me, 'I used to be put off by your superwoman act. You seem softer, more open now. I like you better this way.' "[13]

Cathy, who was single for 10 years after her divorce but who is now remarried, says that her most intimate friendships date from the time right after her divorce. These friends were other divorced women who supported each other out of their shared experiences. Even though Cathy is now happily married, she admits that there are times when she feels nostalgic for the close friendships of that time.

Divorce, then, can either be a time of feeling depressed over lost friendships, or feeling hopeful over building new, more intimate ones. The potential for doing the latter is too great to pass by. The choice is ours.

Building a Support System

 ICE-BREAKER / Groups of 4 to 6 / 15 Minutes

Music in My Life. Go around and let everyone explain this past week—somewhere between the two extremes—in each area of their life. If you do not know the songs, just go with the titles.

IN MY WORK THIS PAST WEEK, IT HAS BEEN ...
Some days the windshield,
some days the bug _____Everything is beautiful

ABOUT MYSELF, I'M FEELING ...
Nobody loves me but my mama,
and she might be lying, too _____Jesus loves me

ABOUT THE FUTURE, I'M FEELING ...
There's a light at the end of the tunnel;   Call me a
I hope it's not a train_____cock-eyed optimist

🖵 RESPOND TO THE VIDEO / Same Groups / 30 Minutes

1. What friendships do you feel you have lost because of your divorce? Why did that happen? How do you feel about losing those friends?

2. In order to develop the kind of friendships you need for a support system, what do you feel you need to do most?
    - ❐ learn to share more openly
    - ❐ get over my shyness
    - ❐ learn how to make small talk
    - ❐ be more vulnerable
    - ❐ be less controlling
    - ❐ free up time in my schedule for friends
    - ❐ "lighten up" and develop more of a sense of humor
    - ❐ learn to ask for help
    - ❐ learn to trust again
    - ❐ develop some new interests
    - ❐ become a better listener
    - ❐ other:_____

3. Finish this sentence: "Right now I need a friend to ..."

4. In making a plan of action for strengthening your friendships, what is the first step you need to take after leaving this group today? How can this group help you take that first step?

The following story was one of Jesus' first miracles, occurring not long after his baptism. It happened in Capernaum which was on the Sea of Galilee, where Jesus did much of his earliest teaching. It was relatively near Nazareth and had become Jesus' second home.

An unusual aspect of this healing was that normally when Jesus healed someone, he said that the faith of the person healed had made him or her well. But in this incident, Scripture credits healing to the faith, not of the healed person, but of the friends of the healed person. Here we see clearly that for a person to be healed, whether the illness is physical, emotional or spiritual, it helps us to not only have faith ourselves, but to be in a community of faith. We need to have friends around us whose faith helps us push forward to find healing. Still, in the end, it was the paralytic himself who had to respond to the call to "get up, take your mat and go home." The friends could not "make him get healed." They could only assist him on his way.

ICE-BREAKER FOR TWO-SESSION OPTION
If you are doing the Bible Study as a separate session, start off this session by dividing the class into small groups of 4 to 6 and answering these questions. Photocopy and give this to the group.

Meal Time. Sometimes we have to take what is served to us. Sometimes we have a choice of what we'll eat.

1. If you were to compare this past week to a meal, what kind of meal would it be?
    ❒ down-home cookin'—filling and good for the soul
    ❒ pheasant under glass—full of elegance, a rare treat
    ❒ pizza with a hot fudge sundae for dessert—lots of fun, but lots of guilt
    ❒ a TV dinner—adequate, but not very exciting
    ❒ dinner at a health food restaurant—probably good for me, but some parts were hard to "get down"
    ❒ a greasy-spoon special—lots of heartburn and a bad taste in my mouth

2. What part of your week was so delectable you just wanted to savor it for a while?

3. What part of your week do you wish you could have "sent back to the chef"?

2 *A few days later, when Jesus again entered Capernaum, the people heard that he had come home. ²So many gathered that there was no room left, not even outside the door, and he preached the word to them. ³Some men came, bringing to him a paralytic, carried by four of them. ⁴Since they could not get him to Jesus because of the crowd, they made an opening in the roof above Jesus and, after digging through it, lowered the mat the paralyzed man was lying on. ⁵When Jesus saw their faith, he said to the paralytic, "Son, your sins are forgiven."*

⁶Now some teachers of the law were sitting there, thinking to themselves, ⁷"Why does this fellow talk like that? He's blaspheming! Who can forgive sins but God alone?"

⁸Immediately Jesus knew in his spirit that this was what they were thinking in their hearts, and he said to them, "Why are you thinking these things? ⁹Which is easier: to say to the paralytic, 'Your sins are forgiven,' or to say, 'Get up, take your mat and walk'? ¹⁰But that you may know that the Son of Man has authority on earth to forgive sins. ..." He said to the paralytic, ¹¹"I tell you, get up, take your mat and go home." ¹²He got up, took his mat and walked out in full view of them all. This amazed everyone and they praised God, saying, "We have never seen anything like this!"

Mark 2:1–12

1. Had you been one of the four friends of the paralytic, and you saw the crowd around where Jesus was, what would you have done?
   ❑ suggested we come back another time
   ❑ politely waited in line
   ❑ figured we were in the right place—good healers, like good restaurants, draw a crowd
   ❑ sent a big tip to the doorman
   ❑ made a hole in the roof, like in the story
   ❑ gone along with a hole in the roof, but made it clear it wasn't my idea

2. How would you have felt if you had been the paralytic when your friends made you "drop in on Jesus" unexpectedly?

3. In your need for healing from the pain of your divorce, what four friends (not including members of this group), could you call on to help you find that healing?

4. As your friends help you to find healing, what is the biggest obstacle they may have to help you overcome?

5. In the end, we must take up our own mats and walk. As you look to your own healing, what is it that after all is said and done, you must do for yourself?

Mark 2:1–12

2:3 *a paralytic.* Any chronic disease or ailment was thought of as a punishment for sin. A paralytic was totally dependent on begging or upon family members to meet his or her needs.

2:4 *an opening in the roof.* The roof of a typical Palestinian house was flat (it was often used for sleeping) and was reached by an outside ladder or stairway. It was constructed of earth and brushwood that was packed between wooden beams set about three feet apart. The roof was easily breached (and easily repaired). A rather large opening would have been required to lower a man on a mat. While this was going on, with the noise and falling dirt, all attention inside would have been diverted from Jesus' sermon to the ever-growing hole.

mat. This was the bed of a poor person.

2:5 *faith.* This is the first time in Mark that this word is used. It increasingly becomes the quality Jesus looks for in those to whom he ministers.

your sins are forgiven. The friends, the man, and the crowd expected a healing; sin was a whole new issue that had not yet been raised by Jesus. This was a deliberate action on Jesus' part to force the religious authorities who were present to grapple with the issue of his identity.

2:6 *teachers of the law.* Literally, "scribes." These were men charged with the responsibility of interpreting and applying Jewish law to the people. They had developed an extensive tradition of interpretation which defined what it meant to keep the Law in all manner of circumstances.

2:7 *blaspheming*. Blaspheming is "contempt for God" and under Jewish law its penalty was death (Lev. 24:16). The teachers of the Law believed that illness was the direct result of sin (e.g. John 9:2), so that the sick could not recover until their sin had been forgiven by God. They also knew that God alone could offer forgiveness. For Jesus to declare this on his own authority was to put himself in the place of God, the vilest form of blasphemy.

2:9 *Which is easier.* Jesus responds to their question (v. 7) in typical rabbinic fashion: he asks them a question. The answer to his question is obvious. It is far easier to say, "Your sins are forgiven," than it is to heal the man right then and there. There is no way to verify whether sins have been forgiven but it is obvious whether a lame man walks or not.

2:10 *But that you may know.* Since healing and forgiveness were linked in their own theology, if Jesus was able to heal the paralytic then the scribes would have to admit that he had, indeed, the power to actually forgive the man's sins. The visible healing would verify the invisible forgiveness. If they were consistent, the teachers of the Law would have to admit that Jesus was at least a representative of God (v. 7).

REBIRTH STARTS WHEN WE DECIDE TO STOP LOOKING AT WHAT HAS DIED...

...AND LOOK TO THE NEW LIFE GOD HAS IN STORE FOR US...

...ACCEPTING AND APPRECIATING SINGLENESS...

...RECLAIMING CONFIDENCE IN MAKING DECISIONS...

...AND SETTING SOME LIFE GOALS FOR WHAT LIES AHEAD...

...IT CAN MEAN A NEW BIRTH!

Looking to the New Life

OBJECTIVES

To see what we must do to put the past behind us and claim what God has for our future.

To reclaim confidence in our ability to make decisions and face challenges.

To look at a passage of Scripture which assures us of God's presence as we face the future.

THREE-PART AGENDA

VIDEO / RESPONSE
20–25 Minutes

BIBLE STUDY
20–25 Minutes

ICE-BREAKER
45 Minutes

NOTE: The agenda is reversed and there is no two-session option.

ICE-BREAKER

We recommend that you use the Ice-Breaker at the close of this session—as part of the evaluation time. This affirmation exercise is on the back of the Handout.

NOTE:
Ice-Breaker
goes last with
Evaluation.

What You Have Helped Me Become. How would you describe your experience with this group? Choose one of the animals below that best describes how your experience in this group affected your life. Then share your responses with the group.

WILD EAGLE: You have helped to heal my wings, and taught me how to soar again.

TOWERING GIRAFFE: You have helped me to hold my head up and stick my neck out, and reach over the fences I have built.

PLAYFUL PORPOISE: You have helped me to find a new freedom and a whole new world to play in.

COLORFUL PEACOCK: You have told me that I'm beautiful; I've started to believe it, and it's changing my life.

SAFARI ELEPHANT: I have enjoyed this new adventure, and I'm not going to forget it, or this group; I can hardly wait for the next safari.

more ⟶

LOVABLE HIPPOPOTAMUS: You have let me surface and bask in the warm sunshine of God's love.

LANKY LEOPARD: You have helped me to look closely at myself and see some spots, and you still accept me the way I am.

DANCING BEAR: You have taught me to dance in the midst of pain, and you have helped me to reach out and hug again.

ALL-WEATHER DUCK: You have helped me to celebrate life—even in stormy weather—and to sing in the rain.

VIDEO SCRIPT

Divorce recovery is as much about the future as the past. Since our divorce, many of us have only been able to see what we have lost. We must—regardless of whether or not we welcomed the divorce—acknowledge and mourn what we have lost. But there comes a point where we must declare that behind us, and look to what God has in store for us. That means three things:

- accepting and appreciating our singleness
- reclaiming our confidence in our decision-making ability
- developing some life goals

Accepting and appreciating our singleness

"They got married and lived happily ever after." We have learned from experience how this fairy tale line can hold a false promise. Marriage does not necessarily bring lasting happiness. Now we must learn another aspect of this falsehood: To be happy we do not have to get married! We can be happy as single persons. We can learn that there are many advantages to not being married. Divorce therapist Bruce Fisher writes:

> A typical comment from a recently separated person might be, "I'll never make it as a single person: I need another love relationship." During the singleness phase (where one has grown comfortable with being single), the same person might say, "Why get married? I can come and go as I please. I can eat whenever I like it. I don't have to adjust my daily living habits to another person. Being single sure feels good!"[14]

Being single does not make us second-class citizens. Sometimes in a world geared to couples, we may feel that way. We have to get married to be "normal" and live a "normal" life. We forget the people who have made their mark in this world living as single adults, not the least of whom were the apostle Paul and Jesus Christ!

Sue

Sue was one who learned that being single could be a good life. When she was first divorced, she looked desperately for a man to love and affirm her, and "make it all better." She found herself allowing men to use her sexually as well as financially. Finally, after several such bad experiences, she asked herself why she was so desperate to find a man. She concluded that it was because she felt she was not whole without one.

Realizing that was an immature idea, she began to see all the advantages she had as a single person, and to affirm herself as a single adult. Sue later told her pastor, "It feels good being free to meet different men and enjoy being with them, without having to 'find a man'!"

Reclaiming our confidence in decision-making

Looking to our new life also means reclaiming confidence in our own ability to make decisions. That confidence has certainly been shaken by our divorce. Some people say that when a person is divorced, it is hard for him or her to trust other people again. While that is certainly true sometimes, it is more often the case that we have trouble trusting our own judgment about other people and about life in general.

Our decision-making capacities had better work, because the reality is that we ultimately have little choice but to trust them again. As Jim Smoke says, "Past failures do not mean future failures unless we have failed to learn from the past."[15]

Setting life goals

Looking to our new life most certainly means setting some life goals for what lies ahead. Goals give a sense of direction to life. In *Alice in Wonderland,* Alice asks the Cheshire Cat, "Would you tell me, please, which way I ought to go from here?" "That depends a good deal on where you want to get to," said the cat. "I don't much care where ..." responded Alice. "Then it doesn't matter which way you go," said the cat. "... So long as I get somewhere," Alice added as an explanation. "Oh, you're sure to do that," said the cat, "if you only walk long enough."[16]

In divorce recovery, too, which way we "ought to go from here" depends on our setting goals for "where we want to get to." Jim Smoke advises divorced people particularly to set goals for themselves in the areas of job, career and money. (He differentiates short-term "jobs" from a long-term "career." The latter contributes to our sense of life purpose.)

Sharon

Sharon, for example, was divorced after five years of marriage. She had married right out of high school and had no marketable skills. She worked as a waitress for a while, but found that to be demeaning and dead-ended. She then set a goal to graduate from college with a more marketable skill. She obtained some loans, made the required sacrifices, and four years later received her degree in education and became a teacher.

A time to die, a time to be born

Looking to our new life, then, will mean something different for each of us. For all of us, however, it can mean a new birth. Rebirth starts when we decide to stop looking at what has died (and pitying ourselves over what we have lost). It develops and forms as we realize that the Creator never stops creating and forming us. It is made complete when, with a trust in our Creator's direction, we focus on the new life God has in store for us.

Looking to the New Life

📺 RESPOND TO THE VIDEO (Groups of 4 to 6 / 20–25 Min.)

1. Which advantage of being single is most important to you?
   - ❐ "one less bell to answer, one less egg to fry"
   - ❐ not having the toilet seat up/down
   - ❐ not having to share my space
   - ❐ coming and going as I please
   - ❐ a more peaceful home
   - ❐ meeting/dating new people
   - ❐ making my own decisions
   - ❐ other:_____

2. In what way, if at all, are single adults sometimes treated as "second-class citizens"? Why does this happen? How much has that affected you?

3. Which do you see as most central to building a new life? Why?
   - ❐ appreciating singleness
   - ❐ regaining confidence in decision-making
   - ❐ setting goals

4. In what area or areas do you most need to develop life goals?
   - ❐ money
   - ❐ self-sufficiency
   - ❐ career
   - ❐ parenting
   - ❐ job
   - ❐ church / faith

📖 RESPOND TO THE BIBLE STUDY (Groups of 4 to 6 / 20–25 Min.)

> *18"Forget the former things;*
>   *do not dwell on the past.*
> *19See, I am doing a new thing!*
>   *Now it springs up; do you not perceive it?*
> *I am making a way in the desert*
>   *and streams in the wasteland."*   Isaiah 43:18–19

1. When and why do people need to forget the past? What "former things" do you need to forget?
   - ❐ bad memories from my marriage
   - ❐ good memories from my marriage
   - ❐ some childhood pain which keeps interfering with my relationships
   - ❐ mistakes I have made which have messed up my life
   - ❐ negative comments people have made about me
   - ❐ other:_____

2. What "new thing" do you see God giving you right now?

This Scripture passage, like the one from Ezekiel in session five, is from the time of Israel's exile in Babylon. During this time, many of Israel's finest citizens—leaders, craftsmen, scholars, etc.—were taken away from their homeland and held captive in a foreign country. Worst of all, they feared they were heading into a frightening future without God. They felt God had abandoned them because of their sin.

In these verses, God beautifully reaffirms his loving relationship with his people. He promises to be with them in any frightening circumstances they might face, as he had been with them in their beginnings as a people.

REFERENCE
NOTES

Isaiah 43:18–19

43:18 *Forget.* Isaiah is not saying the exiles should no longer remember their heritage and history (he has been continually reminding his people about these things). Rather, he is saying, "Stop mournfully looking back and clinging to the past" (Westermann). This same message is also found elsewhere in the Bible: "Do not say, 'Why were the old days better than these?' For it is not wise to ask such questions" (Eccl. 7:10); and "But one thing I do: Forgetting what is behind and straining toward what is ahead, I press on toward the goal to win the prize for which God has called me heavenward in Christ Jesus" (Phil. 3:13b–14).

the former things ... the past. God's earlier acts of redemption, especially the Exodus from Egypt.

43:19 *I am doing a new thing.* God is in the process of doing something now that will be glorious.

a way in the desert. The same "highway" mentioned in Isaiah 40:3, which is to be constructed at God's command for the returning exiles.

streams in the wasteland. This escape route provides a deliberate contrast to Isaiah's earlier prophecy of a wasteland (5:5–10; 6:11) and exile (5:13; 6:12). The message is God's answer to the saying, "Where there's a will, there's a way." Where trouble lies before us, God goes ahead to bring us safely through it.

Looking to the New Life

 ICE-BREAKER / All Together / 45 Minutes (Total)

What You Have Helped Me Become. How would you describe your experience with this group? Choose one of the animals below that best describes how your experience in this group affected your life. Then share your responses with the group.

WILD EAGLE: You have helped to heal my wings, and taught me how to soar again.

TOWERING GIRAFFE: You have helped me to hold my head up and stick my neck out, and reach over the fences I have built.

PLAYFUL PORPOISE: You have helped me to find a new freedom and a whole new world to play in.

COLORFUL PEACOCK: You have told me that I'm beautiful; I've started to believe it, and it's changing my life.

SAFARI ELEPHANT: I have enjoyed this new adventure, and I'm not going to forget it, or this group; I can hardly wait for the next safari.

LOVABLE HIPPOPOTAMUS: You have let me surface and bask in the warm sunshine of God's love.

LANKY LEOPARD: You have helped me to look closely at myself and see some spots, and you still accept me the way I am.

DANCING BEAR: You have taught me to dance in the midst of pain, and you have helped me to reach out and hug again.

ALL-WEATHER DUCK: You have helped me to celebrate life—even in stormy weather—and to sing in the rain.

EVALUATION

Take a few minutes to review your experience and reflect. Go around on each question and share your answers.

1. When you first started this course, how were you feeling?

2. How would you describe the experience of opening up and sharing yourself with this group?

3. What was one of the most significant things you learned?

4. What was the high point in this course for you?

5. What did you appreciate most about the group?

CONTINUATION

Do you want to continue as a group? If so, what do you need to improve? Finish the sentence:

"If I were to suggest one thing we could work on as a group, it would be ... "

MAKE A COVENANT

A covenant is a promise made to each other in the presence of God. Its purpose is to indicate your intention to make yourselves available to one another for the fulfillment of the purposes you share. In a spirit of prayer, work your way through the following sentences, trying to reach an agreement on each statement pertaining to your ongoing life together. Write out your covenant like a contract, stating your purpose, goals, and the ground rules for your group.

1. The purpose of our group will be:

2. Our goals will be:

3. We will meet for _____weeks, after which we will decide if we wish to continue as a group.

4. We will meet from _____ to _____ and we will strive to start on time and end on time.

5. We will meet at _____ (place) or we will rotate from house to house.

6. We will agree to the following ground rules for our group (check):

   ❏ PRIORITY: While you are in the course, you give the group meetings priority.

   ❏ PARTICIPATION: Everyone participates and no one dominates.

   ❏ RESPECT: Everyone is given the right to their own opinion, and all questions are encouraged and respected.

   ❏ CONFIDENTIALITY: Anything that is said in the meeting is never repeated outside the meeting.

   ❏ EMPTY CHAIR: The group stays open to new people at every meeting, as long as they understand the ground rules.

☐ SUPPORT: Permission is given to call upon each other in time of need at any time.

☐ ACCOUNTABILITY: We agree to let the members of the group hold us accountable to the commitments which each of us make in whatever loving ways we decide upon.

☐ ADVICE-GIVING: Unsolicited advice is not allowed.

☐ MISSION: We agree to do everything in our power to start a new group as our mission.

CURRICULUM AND OTHER VIDEO COURSES

Other courses in this series of VIDEO COURSES are listed below. For more information about other group resources and possible direction, please contact your small group coordinator or SERENDIPITY at 1-800-525-9563 or visit us at: www.serendipityhouse.com.

PARENTING ADOLESCENTS: Easing the Way to Adulthood

HEALTHY RELATIONSHIPS: Living Within Defined Boundaries

DEALING WITH GRIEF AND LOSS: Hope in the Midst of Pain

12 STEPS: The Path to Wholeness

MARRIAGE ENRICHMENT: Making a Good Marriage Better

STRESS MANAGEMENT: Finding the Balance

The *Serendipity Bible for Groups* contains a number of Questionnaire Bible Studies. There are two parts to each of these Bible studies. Generally there is no "right" answer to these questions. The answers reflect your understanding and your experience. The name for this sort of small group exercise is relational Bible Study, since the focus is more on the people in the group than on delving deeply into the text. You can do more rigorous Bible Study by using the questions in the margin of the *Serendipity Bible for Groups.*

There is one recovery course for divorce recovery outlined in the *Serendipity Bible for Groups.* In addition what follows are 14 suggested studies—seven from the Old Testament and seven from the New Testament. While these questionnaire studies do not always focus directly on divorce recovery, they all discuss some aspect of the topic. These studies are listed in the order in which they occur in the Bible, not in the order in which you will necessarily want to study them.

Studies From the Old Testament

1. Adam and Eve (Genesis 2:4–25)
   Explore the meaning of intimacy, especially in male-female relationships.

2. The Fall (Genesis 3:1–24)
   Explore what it means to experience moral failure.

3. Jacob and Esau / Isaac's Blessing (Genesis 25:19–34; 27:1–40)
   Explore family conflict and resolution.

4. Joseph Sold by His Brothers (Genesis 37:12–36)
   Explore what it means to feel betrayed by a family member.

5. Joseph Makes Himself Known (Genesis 45:1–28)
   Explore forgiveness and reconciliation in a family setting.

6. Birth and Dedication of Samuel (1 Samuel 1:1–28)
   Explore where we get our feelings of self-worth, in light of Hannah receiving her self-worth from bearing a male child.

7. David and Bathsheba (2 Samuel 11:1–27)
   Explore the reality of sexual temptation.

Studies From the New Testament

1. Parable of the Talents (Matthew 25:14–30)
   Explore the talents God has given you, as part of your effort to establish a new view of self.

2. Jesus Heals and Prays (Mark 1:29–39)
   Explore how to manage the stress in your life and strengthen your relationship with God.

3. Jesus Presented in the Temple (Luke 2:21–40)
   Explore your life direction in relation to your "roots."

4. Jesus Rejected at Nazareth (Luke 4:14–30)
   Explore what it means to feel rejected, in light of Jesus' rejection.

5. Parable of the Lost (Prodigal) Son (Luke 15:11–32)
   Explore your own "journey from home" in relation to that of the prodigal.

6. Jesus Changes Water to Wine (John 2:1–11)
   Explore your hope for a new beginning.

7. The Woman Caught in Adultery (John 7:53–8:11)
   Explore your need to forgive yourself and accept God's forgiveness.

ENDNOTES:

[1] Elisabeth Kübler-Ross, *On Death and Dying* (New York: MacMillan Publishing Co., 1969).
[2] Jim Smoke, *Growing Through Divorce* (Eugene, OR: Harvest House Publishing, 1976), p. 35.
[3] Maria Sullivan, *The Parent/Child Manual on Divorce* (New York: RGA Publishing Group, 1988), p. i.
[4] Bruce Fisher, *Rebuilding: When Your Relationship Ends* (San Luis Obispo, CA: Impact Publications, 1981), p. 20.
[5] Jim Smoke, *Growing Through Divorce* (Eugene, OR: Harvest House Publishing, 1976), p. 29).
[6] Ibid., p. 99.
[7] First reported in Keith Madsen, *Fallen Images: Experiencing Divorce in Ministry* (Valley Forge, PA: Judson Press, 1985), p. 76
[8] First reported in William Bridges, *Transitions* (Reading, MA: Addison-Wesley Publishers, 1980), p. 95.
[9] Bruce Fisher, *Rebuilding: When Your Relationship Ends* (San Luis Obispo, CA: Impact Publications, 1981), p. 98.
[10] Dennis and Matthew Linn, *Healing of Memories* (New York: Paulist Press, 1984), p. 15.
[11] Jim Smoke, *Growing Through Divorce* (Eugene, OR: Harvest House Publishing, 1976), p. 28.
[12] Diane Vaughan, *Uncoupling* (New York: Oxford University Press, 1986), p. 145.
[13] Alan Loy McGinnis, *The Friendship Factor* (Minneapolis, MN: Augsburg, 1979), p. 28.
[14] Bruce Fisher, *Rebuilding: When Your Relationship Ends* (San Luis Obispo, CA: Impact Publications, 1981), pp. 182–183.
[15] Jim Smoke, *Growing Through Divorce* (Eugene, OR: Harvest House Publishing, 1976), p. 72.
[16] Lewis Carroll, *Alice in Wonderland* (Grosset and Dunlap, Inc., 1946), pp. 66–67.